LINES OUT

LINES OUT

Poems by

ROSAMOND ROSENMEIER

ALICE JAMES BOOKS

Cambridge, Massachusetts

Library of Congress Cataloguing-in-publication Data
Rosenmeier, Rosamond, 1928
I. Lines Out.
PS3568.0826L56   1989   811'.54—dc20
Library of Congress #89-14855
ISBN 0-914086-88-X (paper)

Printed in the United States of America
This book has been set in Goudy Old Style at
The Writer's Center, Bethesda, Maryland
Cover illustration and design by Vickie Schafer

ACKNOWLEDGMENTS

Some of these poems, or earlier versions of them, first
appeared in the following publications: *The Carlton Miscellany*
("American Directions"); *Epoch* ("The April 1st Visit to the
Seed Store of the Eastern States Farmers Cooperative"); *The
Nation* ("Poetry No One Reads", "Pumpkin", "Walden Changes");
New Mexico Quarterly ("Currants and Ferns", "Local Bird"); *The
Virginia Quarterly Review* ("Learning the Songs of Birds").

Grateful acknowledgment is also made to Alfred A. Knopf for
permission to use the sentence "Without thee, O Sophia, what
value has anything?" from *Letters of Wallace Stevens*, ed.
Holly Stevens, 1966, p. 625.

I would like to thank the poets of Alice James Books for their
help in preparing this manuscript.

The publication of this book was made possible with support from
the Massachusetts Council on the Arts and Humanities, a state
agency whose funds are recommended by the Governor and
appropriated by the State Legislature.

Alice James Books are published by the Alice James Poetry
Cooperative, Inc., 33 Richdale Avenue, Cambridge, MA 02140

For Jesper,

and for Jason, Twyla, Alan, Peter, and Leah

Listening for you
makes me think of distances.

CONTENTS

I. Here.

II. A Postcard for Anne Bradstreet

III. Currants and Ferns

IV. December Coming In

I. HERE

Here

On roads west,
some tar, some dirt,
headlights wink
through the dark grass
past a twilight clothes-
line of cold socks,
a shed door open.
At the curb
a blue Plymouth is stopped dark:
stickers on its bumper say
Permit to Park and *Polar Caves*.

Here a small house
holds its driveway to its side
while through the fenceless yard
a cement walk straightens to the door;
shadowed by hydrangeas
a man sits on wood porch steps.
Inside the screen an electric light is on
and at the curb
a mailbox lid opens down
like a can opened for dinner:
on its metal
the printing of a name.

Watering

Evening after evening
calls me out. My soul
sometimes still in its apron
or in its housedress comes
wiped with biscuit dough,
its hands sometimes
crushed on with raspberries,
or yellowed, tangy
from the tying of tomato vines.
It smells of its soil,
my soul, and its arms are feathered
with seeds of grass, corn tassels,
milkweed. Cut grass
sticks with mud
in its garden sandals.

It voyages down the path
just at nightfall,
pulling the hose to seedlings;
the yellow dog who goes with me
follows beside it.
Gnats and mosquitoes desire us.
This week seven of my bees at once
stung my ankles in anger.
Am I not, then, admixed with nature?
And my soul, now nursing,
now angering, now watering,
is it not involved in the perfect life of instinct?

Behind, in milky porchlight,
wait the three in pale pajamas
who call and carry on to get me to come back,
while here deep in shadow
I kneel to put the nozzle down,
and my knees take the imprint of pebbles.
Then standing up unsandaled,
both bare feet step — like that —
into the dark cloud, the seeping down
softly, of water.

I Have Gone Up

into this yes
damn paradise,
not now, not ever, never
to lie again in my stony home
and the same sky that
blesses me with rain
spatters my city's
airless old window
facing nameless neighbors,
while this cloud cover, plain
like my stone yard,
grieves me
for a look of street,
for gaunt-eyed flats
starved straight down
to the kiss and stroke of lovers
twined in black knots
above the river, dark,
churning light and stars.

Poetry No One Reads

Black summer trees. Sky lemon blued.
The house dead in sleep.
A far barking in the late light
I cannot understand
But jot down: Staccato of dogs.
And sometimes simply the noise of myself
Barks in the late light.

Janot's Keepsake

Still I keep this sight of dockmen
setting guard rails into place, while
far in haze, not yet seen, the ship
moves through the distant mouth. Then seen,
serious, slow, criss-crossed by wakes
of small craft, she clears the stiff bank
and berths at the caverned pier where
I stand in the crowd gathering.
My young bones, my dress, shake against
the fence, waiting. Bolts of sun strike
her sudden decks. Along her rails
passengers have come into view.
Your shouts flood from the canopy
into this dim room, disembarked,
where my arms now hold your shadow.
You stand still in love's dead surprise.

Rock grove, skyward island, the horned
hive of the city, where night's black
rainscraps, its moonless air, our breath,
are caught, our eyes caught, wandering
the wet streets eastward. The lights like
leafwork, like glassy petals, fall.
The bridges move beaded in the
river's black water. Clouds let down
their canopies. Sparks fall. Stars fall
and the bright dense nectars of
memory are making and made.

Lines Out

We window on this
new snow — snow like moon sand
stiffened where it fell.
The white sheet covers
a black midden;
it shrouds a darkness
of shells, leaves,
insects, old bones,
chips of china.

Stars bed cold
in darkness overhead.
Clear to the road
through black air
swing thin wires
pole to pole —
live threads
connecting street to house
under the heavy threat of branches.

We chance it here at zero,
tune our sets,
draw light and heat
from tenuous silver cords —
lines that will unlink us
when they break.

Alhambra Landscape

i.

In the photo, a tomboy,
tall for her seven years,
brown hair bobbed straight, clasped in a tight barrette;
her dress is starched and ironed.
On the back:
"June. Alhambra, California. 1935."

She lives across the street from Mr. Johnson's
grapefruit orchard (off-limits).
Beyond it, in heavy spice air
the ragged eucalypti guard the riverless riverbed
where bone-white rocks burn
but at night cool and move with shadow.
The arroyo is what the riverbed is called.

One of the voices in the kitchen says,
"Time to go out and play now."
Her high-top brown shoes take her down the walk
through the wood gate.
Up the street in the third house
lives her friend, her big friend, Elizabeth.

Across the arroyo, in San Gabriel, the carnival is set up.
She can hear it. The music plays round and round,
"O-O-O, and it comes out here."
At night in bed she listens to what the song says.
She thinks it's a song about bathroom things.

She turns up the street to meet Elizabeth
who is called half-wit.
She has breasts. She is Catholic.
She smells (The nuns have a dry smell, with sweat in it).
Elizabeth's mother is deaf and her father isn't home.
Elizabeth doesn't go to school.

The two friends hold hands to cross the street,
stepping through the vacant lot
out onto the overgrown banks of the arroyo.
Here and there, the cactus has a salmon flower.
In winter flood time, wood scraps, tin cans, bottles
wash down, and that's what they also call it: the wash.

Cicadas make the air grainy with scraping,
and the tossed rocks lie like chalk.
Elizabeth says not to come here at night.
She says this is where the tramps sleep,
and that it's time to go home now.

ii.

In September second grade starts and
the time for walks is past.
After lunch recess, her class files
into the long corridor to the classroom
where Sister shuts the door.
In a starched uniform,
still outside, she crouches by the wall.
Above her, the St. Teresa church bell rings one o'clock.
She slips out through the north gate
and runs on the dust,
breathless along the road to the trestle,
climbs through it, over into a hollow nest of sand.

When she tells Sister she just wanted to see
how far the wash went,
and Sister isn't mad,
she thinks it's because she's Protestant and
Protestants (Sister says) don't make it to Heaven anyway.
But Elizabeth cried and said not to do that anymore.

iii.

In second grade she is learning
that certain things matter.
At home it matters how you talk.
If she talks back,
her mother tells her father on the phone.
When he gets home from work, he takes off his shoe
and beats her with it. That's called spanking.

Afterwards, she lies in bed stone-still,
her sheet pulled over her face
so that no one can find her.
The round carnival song sounds; she thinks the tramps
are listening in the sand hollow,
and that tomorrow she will tell Elizabeth
she heard angels sitting on her roof
just above her window where the sycamore
leans down almost touching it.
Maybe that will stop Elizabeth's crying.
And then her own large sobs come,
heaving the still stuck boards,
the far trash to an angry stop.
Along the arroyo
torn bodies of the eucalyptus
toss their wild hair, guarding
in sleep all that is unsaid still.

II. A POSTCARD FOR ANNE BRADSTREET

A Postcard For Anne Bradstreet

— May 11, 1657 . . . Many refreshments have I
found in this my weary pilgrimage, and in
this valley of Baca many pools of water . . . .
(Anne Bradstreet)

May 11, 1980 . . .

Pigeons' wings heave as the flock
cruises the garage, lighting in a cluster
just on the edge of the roof.

In this city yard *have I found refreshment.*
The boy next door, barely seen through bridal wreath,
sits lost on his back porch,
playing the radio.

This afternoon a muddy pool forms on the path
from the hose at our back door,
leaking because the washer is old.
Cautious of the drips, a robin
dares to drink there. He nods.
His bright bold eye meets mine.

Many refreshments have I found
in this my weary pilgrimage, and
in this valley of Baca many pools of water.

Upstairs the young couple whose bedroom
shades are pulled
do not make a sound.

Pumpkin

After the pollen powdered yellow flower
under fan leaves, under thick palms
on far watery stems
lying passionate yards out
deep in summer gone,
the pumpkin heaves
big belly and thigh
up from the brown grass —
August's ghost, whose smart orange sun
smacks the frost dark field

Thick skin, full of seed,
every shell *keeps Peter's* wife —
gold ripe rind, unkept mealy flesh
boiled in the pot for vegetable or pie,
or, in the long warm autumn oven,
baked into custard and crust;
the salted seeds toast like nuts
while the outer shell stands by.

Every part used, teeth carved,
smile carved hollow as a gesture,
her crooked candle eyes
haunt at the doorstep.
A gala one night flame glows
through the brief mask;
most orange in that persona,
she burns alive as that wry artifact.

April 1st Visit to the Seed Store of the Eastern States Farmers Cooperative

Up the loading platform, past peat
in bales, limestone and buckwheat sacks,
through the seedsman's door, into deep
barn air as dry as libraries —
I cross the floor; every board greets
a kitchen gardener not at ease
with farmers — the wintry few just
stand like old statues, dim, absorbed.
From my purse I unfold my list:
one-half pound *Progress* — early peas.
Seneca — corn, July, big ears
sun grown from golden ancestries.
I read each pack on its long hook —
Straightneck, Sugar Baby, Blackspine —
names we daily peel, slice and cook.
The March eyes of the man behind
the counter turn blue as he leans
out (Emerson, I'll call him), hands
me his picture catalogue of green
come-ons, an ideal bright harvest
that says, *Local Soil Will Grow These.*
Under a broad hat, Walt at rest
by the window, muses skyward;
hands in pockets, not serious
about planting, he'll rather watch
me when I plant mine, curious.

And among the bean packets, one
who knows beans and celebrates corn,
grumbling at labels in sour tones,
impatient to finger the seed
itself. I step forward with mine
to be added. All told, I've bought
three dollars and sixty cents worth —
too much for my small garden plot.
Seeds keep, he says, if dry and cold.
Worried there may be more to ask,
needing the printed help I hold,
I see the others, timeless, stout.
They know seed. They move slow. Were they
to buy, they'd throw the packets out.

Walden Changes

Shore, public hut site,
your hearth's grave place —
the literal monument remains,
bathed in the sunsmoke
of October afternoon.
Like water birds
last dappled leaves fly down
sinking to seem fish.
The limbs of white birch drown
pallid in clear water.
All relics are collected
and the beach is closed:
soundless, except your western Atropos,
clack-clack, now diesel,
disappears bankrupt to Fitchburg.
Now's too cold for bees to make new honey;
they winter in the hive
and there consume the old.
So we sip your morning words
addressed to us exactly.
Walden: in the reliquary of its print
the tongues of summer gather;
liquid sounds ripen there and change.
Something of you unseals, breathes out,
walks into our air —
a cranky mood, its homespun pockets
scratchy, full of nails.
You come through hedge and stubble
to perform all parts
in a practical allegory,
each stage set with its antipodes;

for prompters you plant the ancients
on these young banks,
while the native woods crowd in.
All acts pool into the round
of a single scene, doubling out in ripples
that touch no shore they yet diminish to.
In that scene
the sole self at center
confronts its many selves,
seasonal selves, like costumes,
changing rapidly as light —
extravagant dissemblances:
Troy put on, pretences of Delphi,
now holy water dipped with the priest of Brahma,
now a studied mime of the wintry Cenobite.
And, for entr'acte, a simultaneous bold burlesque —
beans, bells, firesteed and frogs —
personae for a wise poor fool
who keeps no king,
and tells the prophecies of owls.
While, from the wings,
you watch as well,
a man without fit self to cover,
pale, trying the moult of these garments,
looking in the green glass of the blue water.
Which is how we watch
and what we watching are.
Nothing worn is warm enough
in the dark change coming.

No light is light enough,
but you so fix our eyes
that we see night with morning in it;
you make its cold warm,
a moth of its worm,
a leaf lapse from the globe of its bud.
Something of us
winters your grave possibilities
and wings alive into the present air.

American Renaissance: The Day The Machine Broke

The Puritan reactor —
that bust, old
non-fiction
generator,
worn faucet, bolt, fan,
suction and function —
did sort of work
this morning:
pump ticking,
box talking,
on thin
Messianic treads.

But then
some sort of
regulator went.
Afternoon spent it,
and how
the steam let blow!
Figurations rode the air —
no specifications given.
Yee-ipes, the boys said
watching poetical ghosts fly
from the sheer exhaust.

Emerson's Sheets

Alone and aimless
through tense bright January air,
my car takes me cruising
past, as Emerson said, his *gate*. There,
in the side yard hang two bed sheets, publicly
pinned tight, frozen stiff like boards.
Staunch cottons, they hang as if standing up against
the gusts that whip and drain them dry.

My mind clings and fastens to that sight.
How such sheets would have pleased our forgoer Emerson.
Consider the nonchalance. . ., he would have said.
See how they, resisting, catch the sun
and bounce it back. *They are all sail. . . moth wings. . .*
a *daily web of new relations.*

I and my car park and make the *shadow*
of a passing traveler. He would have said,
these draperies are the *splendid masks of being.*
They are *enough;* we need *no further proof*
that the past is always swallowed and forgotten;
whatever the calamity, *it has been caused to fade and disappear*
as an *early cloud of insignificance.*
These are the *veils that shut down the facts of tomorrow.*
With these we need *no description of the countries towards which we sail.*

I see that Emerson's fiery cottons are without stain;
no sour privacies yet cling,
wept in the sickness of his child's dying,
no spots —

nothing indelible of the widower Emerson
lying on his mucus and hair.
How completely I have triumphed over these black events,
Emerson said, in the manner of giving us a gift.

Such fatherly white flights are a deadly shock,
as cold and bright as those events were black.
I can no longer, as I start the car, stand this hope;
it is a *bleached picture*, an *effigy* merely.
I look away. Moving on helps me to *pierce* this *rotten diction*,
yet in my ear his words resound,
bruised and broken, this time a venerable *tapestry*,
viewed as if from the other side — dim, knotted, pieced,
the way he did not want it seen.
In my mouth his words loosen and fade.
When they turn ragged,
the obverse weave of my days, too, shows through.

It is then that
my car becomes *machine without escape,*
spontaneous;
my experience blends with the *present action of my mind.*
I drive straight but blind into the view
where a dark gust clouds and stirs the air,
as from moist giant wings,
looming and beating.

That gust is a fit likeness
of Emerson's true calling.
The ghostly effort of those wings
bespeaks a threadbare testament
to a *world* that *is emblematic* still.

Earthsurface Dawned with Presences

Without thee, O Sophia, what value has anything?

Wallace Stevens

I.

With ruddiness, with blue and feathered skies,
the world rests in its dawn, while earthen beneath
a stout woman of hidden virtue lies.

Let no one say what will become her
or what she will become.

Stretched in starched frock and muddied brogues westward,
blind to the hills darkening her morning,
she sleeps hard in New England pastures.

Further east, rainstorms at sea; in Boston,
green balloons. The day prepares parades.
The air turns in gala revolutions.

What tittering pulse, what lusty rumor
scuds over her tired eyes into
the well-tuned ears of Amos? No sooner

does he reach a near nook of her icy field
than, red-faced old comedian, he shoves
grey snow off her sombre sides. Will she yield

to that wry poke? Smiles crack, warm humors run
with change; her stony winter habits
melt to jade guffaws. Selah, old bawd of sun.

II.

In red, white and starry diamond skies
this dawn has cannoned up, while brown beneath
in hopsacking our native mother lies.

Her sod fades, legendary, westward,
while the frosty eastern hills keep morning
from her dark encrusted shroud of pasture.

Let no one say what will become her
or what she will become.

Meanwhile east, at sea, somewhere past Boston,
dim "Ka-boom-boom"; the day prepares parades.
Why do these ructions of Revolution

not pulse within her hearing? Such rumors
as here scud pothole pools whisper only to
the captive ears of boys. No sooner

at the corner of the lowland field
than, red-necked, in worn cocoons, they shove
each other off old snow, thumb a ride, yield

to the first Ford city-bound. Her sons run
off to change stale poplin winter habits
for faded uniforms and tricks of sun.

III.

With weakest tints of awakening skies
this dawn comes faintly clarion. Beneath,
barely in light, a plain young woman lies.

Let no one say what will become her
or what she will become.

A patchwork covers her, stretching westward
while she dozes, unwilling that morning
should, quite yet, disrupt the quiet pastures

of the sea where she dreams. In Boston
balloons float and the day prepares parades.
For her what pastoral revolution

pulses with insinuating rumor
across a simple brow? What warmth slips into
her slumbering dark thought? No sooner

does she feel day touch the earliest field
than she reddens, awakening to shove
off old snow, to break from frost and yield

herself to change. Lightfall overruns
her nakedness, weaving a brief, sweet habit,
soon jaded by the touches of the sun.

Let no one say what will become her
or what she will become.

IV.

With light more auroral than these skies
a dawn occurs. The original beneath
turns towards that influence, dreaming as she lies

of sensuous pageantries spread westward
from this set stage of hills; her morning
of the imagination makes pastures

of the sea. A solid man of Boston
sits in furnished rooms, awaiting old parades,
deaf to the sound of fresher revolutions.

Or does his pulse record this wild, winged rumor
scudding across our sky, lighting into
the hemlocks? There the lone songster, sooner

than dawn, feels dawn. She wakes the field
red with maple bloom. A faint new shove
of air heralds the fact of birds; she yields

to summer's mood, announcing she's done
encumbrances. Her ancient habit
turns jade again. It answers back with sun.

Let no one say what will become her
or what she will become.

Peter Reading

After school,
Peter, age five,
waits in the small alcove,
Indian-style on the carpeted floor,
books strewn, reading one
under the sharp light falling
on his cornstook hair,
down the back of his pale neck,
collarless shirt, blue sweater —
his new dark blue sweater, I notice,
as I step across the threshold.

"How come you took so long?" he says, not looking up.

"The traffic was bad. I had to wait for the bus.
C'mon now. Let's get going."

He keeps on turning pages,
his boots tucked under the book on his lap,
his head working back and forth,
all the way to the very end. Slowly.
He hasn't learned to read yet.
So, what his mind does, led on by the book,
I do not know.
What story is there for him to know
before he can read it?
I am here, but not here.
He is somewhere, not here,
not yet reading, but in a story.

"There," he says.
"I'll just put these away so they won't get stepped on."

Of Joyce Horner

Mt. Holyoke College: 1944-1968

What she spoke
at times secluded
in such brief disclosures
I could not catch to know.
Or sometimes her eyes
hurried as from our countryness
to look out only,
as if preferring an interior
perhaps more native.

But now see
where at this distance
I have tacked her verse
to hang my walls.
How it windows them open
out to an historic garden
visible through summer shapes of shade;
a fine transparence haunts and warms
falling its light in leaves
simply, as the sun in air.

The border of her allegory
runs thick, elaborate, alive with voices
like a hedge with birds.
While back beyond suggests a sort of wilderness;
there the satisfying savage roams unseen,
cavorts and feeds,
and yields himself to her firm idiom.

Local Bird

He lights down
from the pine grove
onto the window feeder,
Capped black wit,
smug puffed black ascot,
sharp eye brought brief to a point
he pecks to break a shell.

The window glass between us
protecting him he thinks,
he chat chats, chews, picks,
spits a seed,
then boldly bursts his chicka-dee-dee-dee,
tilting his head
to study the inflections.

While he eats
he seems to consider something,
frowning —
at some nut bit?
Some cat current snatched in weeds?
Or, dee-dee,
a portent in the bug he bites?

Some intimacy quivers him.
He nods, jumps terse to the edge,
looks farewell facing air,
and on some signal dives
like light,
splashing directly into it.

American Directions

Even so, I like to look at pictures of European streets.
A certain angle of the lens
seems to narrow my gaze down them,
between the buttressings, past crookedness,
past antiquities, past even trees and stone,
into the deep-alleyed eye of time, its well,
a darkness at the center of the scene.

In that darkness I sometimes see a kind of history,
a seduction of forms and difficult philosophies,
where the continent of Europe appears an aged chanteur
who dominates my continent with his old design —
her wild unkempt hair hills and plains
all natural and unstyled,
even in that moment, Leda-like, ravishing.

Which, of course, no one expected was to last.
From the sour odor of gossip:
how she devoted herself to the children solely,
made them young Americans and grew slovenly herself;
how he deserted her, turning back to his own interests;
and how she thinks now only of her household in the future,
and claims for her grandchildren
those great expanses out Main Street past the end of town.

I more than look into these European streets,
I try them on — that wine, its tongue,
those tastes darkening
until I am beside myself to feel the whispered
old worn lyric in his face.
But I cannot more meet that distant eye
than with this backward glance;
the way I turn to take is pathless, if more real.

III. CURRANTS AND FERNS

Currants and Ferns

Unnatural for me,
it feels like craning my neck
to recognize an absolute.
In the old orchard the other Sunday morning
I saw what looked like one —
a circle of light inside my eyelids
when I closed them — a white
that moved away as if to disappear.
I wasn't trying for absolutes;
I just happened to close my eyes that tight
because pulling ferns out of the currants
is hard work.

When we first moved to this garden,
the ferns were green, tropical, high like palms,
Mediterranean jungle flown feathers
flocking this far sour soil
where unnoticed currants grow.
Someone said that years ago
this was a man-high fern valley
where persons walking through fell
faint from the sweet heavy odor.
But no one said we would wake seeing
one morning not green but rusted fronds
July had burnt brown like fall.

And it was also said that ferns have
a special kind of not true root.
Whatever they have latches them down
into the dirt so hard it takes
all my full grown weight on the rake
to pry up and tear them out.

Not only weight, but slow skill
to get the whole clump up without
parts broken off.

When the great wad of fern comes suddenly unclung
spattering my face, I wipe
and watch for worms
unhoused on the turned over underside,
and this confirms what I suspected — that
the serpent came out of the ferns,
not down from the trees.

For the trees are, in my old orchard,
still the place of angels; their rope knotted,
they climb their unseen voices
out to the farthest branch of the branch,
swinging down or lying there
giving the signal to blast off.
Tests, dangers, countdowns
rolling out of the trees
in sounds blossoming the air,
like petals down onto grass.

Now that we have lived through all the seasons here,
I can hold aside fern and find the red gems,
hidden, where the value is —
the light and dark of liquid beads
veined, clustered, lighter than,
on the Christmas table half a year away,
the tart currant abstract of sun
and green and air
restored, absolved, made firm.

Hello

for Leah

This poem should be born the sudden way you were:
whole and healthy, like a kiss hello.
Not that it should at once sit up, or say words, or walk,
but that it should have all ten toes on its slant feet;
it should suck its small breath,
and move its lips as if kiss-making,
and it should tremble the yet moist lids of its eyes,
half-open, in half-sleep.

It had started to snow. I could feel you coming — that low tight pain. I neatened the front room and put a wash in. Then I lay down. Peter and Alan climbed up beside me to feel my stomach tighten. "Sh-h," they said, and then to your muffled moving, "There!" A knee? A shoulder? A heel? Twyla and Jason did their homework so that they could take care of things if we had to go to the hospital. I got up and made dinner: pork and noodles. Everyone ate. Then I lay down again. I said to Papa that we'd better go. My bag was half-packed and I put the last things in. At the door we all hugged; then I climbed into the microbus. Papa drove carefully. It was slippery. He said, "You're not saying anything." I said, "I'm having contractions." When we got to the hospital, I said I'd better not try to walk. Papa ran through the entrance and came back with a nurse and a wheel-chair. Inside, they said, "She's crowning!" as they lifted me from the chair to the stretcher and ran, all in one motion. The delivery room doors swung open. Over onto the birth bed, feet in stirrups. Those bright lights and clean sheets. But Papa had to wait outside (rules in those days).

As I looked to catch sight of him through the door, the
doctor rushed in tying his mask, and you, with one large
push at the doctor's coaching, were born. Plump, I
thought. A girl person, you were almost called your
grandmother's name; just a shadow of "Harriet", left behind
for the name, "Leah".

There, I have just been in birth with you again.
And when I see you a block away — stepping off the bus
lugging your blue duffel, swinging your way
towards me in old sneakers,
and when you sing out,
there I am again.
And there you are:
sudden and spontaneous, like a kiss hello.

Griefwork for my Mother

You seem to me to be again as if
alive and near, in the room just beyond
the stairs, where traces of a child's piano
wrinkle the air.

I find it no different, still waiting at
your door. Have you dozed off, low radio on,
amidst the other murmurs of the house,
window shades drawn?

I lose the sense of where you are. The tense
quiet in the house still expects your cough.
And that familiar silence down the hall,
is that, again, you?

Alan's June Bug

Early Alan
rocked into the bathroom
with the fuzz of sleep still on
and stopped:
June bugs,
hitting the light all night,
had dropped into the tub —
stunned brown shells dying at dawn
or slipping, inching on the porcelain.

None escape.
Some are tipped onto their backs
wearing themselves out pushing
wild legs at air;
one, rightside up,
is moving towards the drain.
"He'll get sucked down!" cries Alan,
whose reach halts
at the prickly thought of bugs' legs;
bravely though,
he takes it by the back
and lifts it up.

Rescued,
now in a jar
exalted and all day
gravely carried everywhere,
it has been told secrets,
fed grass, rattled
and listened to;
we can't tell
if he knows it's died;
he won't let on.

Learning the Songs of Birds

In the black bright city
all my birds slept as they grew.
Between moist brick their summer throats wintered
traced like seed in the grave familiar stone,
then in rows of wing burst up into trees,
in flocks showering down onto grass.
Always the nameless birds looked to wing free
from, yet towards themselves, finding.

Now summer after summer
songs mass our shade,
their invisible confusions thick as country leaves —
a crowd of local noise I cannot name. Even the common
twenty-five on the record of bird calls you gave me
seem dialects of a foreign — no, of a native tongue
I have to work to know.
The other afternoon I put the record on
when a sudden phrase of lilacs spilled
in the cool of a May garden
walled behind the old inn.
Rain jewels the little tables just put down
until the waiter comes to wipe them off.
The sign reads "Garden now open"
but only we sit out. Across the rainy grass
the low sun, clearing and warm, sheds its rose.
In the moist iced glass, each, an olive,
May green. From that moment's point
of eyes, of fingertips,
the melody falls in sweet bursts.
Nightingale I would have guessed.
But no. Of course.
I learn Robin.

Knowledge begun, I put the record on again
now listening not to a common twenty-five
But to my own to waken them.

In full sun, we step out into Connecticut
fallow morning, rocks deep in weeds.
The odor of coffee perks through the screen door.
Up the hill a sudden thrush dives,
splashes gone into oaks.
At the table in the arbor, bacon, muffins, peach jam;
we talk, eat, fill the day.
Breathless over us, the thrush follows
to upper fields for huckleberries, wild grapes,
blueberries mixed in the picking.
Back to our grass we set the pails down
washing purples clear and chill in well water.
The berries float. We scoop them up.
Overhead the thrush floats his trills, his stops.
All the long humid afternoon
the kerosene stove sputters under a pungent jelly.
We lie and wait for it. Flies bite.
The jelly poured, we bathe on the grass
in late sun, in cold tubs, as the thrush lifts and
drops his song like clear water,
singing us farther and farther into dusk.

The day has gone cool.
The solemn cuckoo haunts the limbs
and recesses of the sour woods next door;
her tone sucks summer from the air.

I try to turn away the sound
which melts into the dissonance of this later yard;
costlier colors ripen into newer chords,
raw without memory. Along the woods edge ground
the scratch and hop of the rufus towhee,
cognac brown, satin white and black.

Silvery rings the veery
high above shrill voices arguing their games.
The oriole mocks at us, his golden apple breast
crowning the tree where he eats.
Our patch of sky shreds in gashes orange, scarlet, blue —
flicker, tanager, bluejay. I slowly learn
the bold mixed consummation of the August air.

Among those yet unlearned remain
dark future birds I can identify
but dread to waken. The pee-wee, before dawn,
lonely dark and small cries in the night,
and well into dusk the screech owl
mourns a knowledge he completes, alone
of all our birds, nearer and nearer
until he falls from sound.

Jason

Like summer's leaves, the sweet fat days have
been thinned from those legs running bases;
those knobby tall stalks plant themselves at third
collecting all their strength to make it home.

As the winey songs of these babblers wild
in leaves will go with the summer that hides them,
and clear small winter birds come, familiar,
a few, for seed at the expected times,

so went the tickling under ears, the mouth games
and soft idiot noises, wet and wordless,
the nectary toes sucked like thumbs,
wiped from the woodwork, as fall and winter

rooms grow neater, more articulate.
Their air distills sunlight. A thin compass
of boy's legs shadows the floor — taller
by all that goes, by all that gives away.

Uses of Loss

for Harriet and Herbert Rauch

The garden's stormed and grave
with damage. Brown sunflakes
fertile ashes of leaves
reel down and faint awash,
their bronze rained and blown frail.
I stand with you this midst
of earth-transacting rose,
this warp of winter light
that's worked the flesh of shade
clear down to distances.
Time to mound up these piles
for use in other weathers.
Steadying the child in me,
I rake what's left to burn,
to feed. Whatever
cannot be borne away
waits here to break, at last,
into fire. Cracklings blur
the late blue afternoon
in slow smoke; the red licks
yield a kind of harvest.
Whitening the bare stalks,
fire flares and falls with sounds
my eye saves like seed: flames,
coals, gems, ash: Here, take them
before your earth burns out.

Long Distance Call to my Daughter, Twyla, May 1975

I've left a message
that your flight cannot be confirmed.
This is a long distance call,
all the way back from both our childhoods:
mine first, in the desert
where you now live,
and yours concluding
as you now inwardly revisit it,
seeking something of yourself
which you were not given,
and you will not find.
Ours is a strange transplanting:
I East, you West.
You are in my childhood's landscape;
I, daily, in yours.

I cannot tell you not to look for shade.
I am a Californian; you come from desert soil.
I wept for the shade of all things not given —
it is a dry labor, my inheritance.
I asked forgiveness.
Exiled and in flight,
I sought permission.
May the rock, the latent garden
of that concluded time
be blessed.

I have called to say that no confirmation is given.
Yet there is eastwardness and westwardness
sufficient to you as an arc and source.

You will bring down rainwater into the lemon groves.
You will irrigate for palms, and in time,
contain your own mother and father;
their broken covenant will break alive in you.
Your lemon groves will flower and bear
and shade you, for a little while.
Blessed be.

Safe Harbors

In the damp far corner of my aunt's patio,
the snail behind the jade plant
is, I think, deciding.

The morning air is California fog-cool.
The sprinklers have been on;
the cement is still moist enough for travel.

Horns up, sensors down, the snail's head
points north, then south.
It is possible, yet, to cross over

to the safety of wet grass —
except for the crack that extends
like an ant arroyo, dividing patio from the walk beyond.

A snail's soft, sticky underfoot
must not like the sting and tackle
of the tiny black traffickers along that crack.

Another place where snails house and wait
is up the side of the patio wall,
where the under-edges of the rough tan bricks

give shade — a cool haven, even in noon sun.
But already the bricks to be climbed are dry;
the wall's nooks and porches now are out of reach.

And under the lips of pots —
the smooth, wet, mossy ones — are also
where snails go, fitted tight, in a beaded row.

I never see snails on their ways there.
I see them after they've arrived:
the golden spiral bone, precious pin-wheels,

stuck like whelks on sea rocks.
Or snails go deep between the prongs of the healing plant:
they line the skin of the lime-green chutes,

crowding down them, horns drawn in,
defended by the spiked edges of the aloe.
They harbor there close to the night-damp ground, all day.

IV. DECEMBER COMING IN

December Coming In

You are knocking with a great knock,
and I am running down the long stairs all the way
to open the front door, unlatched,
pulled — like that — wide to you:
firm standing, pleased with yourself, where twined
on each post of the lintel the euonymous climbs over,
evergreen stems almost trees, hanging
with red berries in this season.

The sun behind you blinds me while I stand believing
you have pulled off your gloves
and stepped over the threshold.
All the sun thrusts in with you,
flooding the fire's hearth, the walls,
the hall floor shining, until,
like chandeliers, all my candles burn,
and the wine is poured, is poured.

Relations

Sitting here writing
in this upstairs room, I expect you home.
Listening for you
makes me think of distances.
I remember gazing from airplanes
and how everyone flying feels the loss of touch.
It always helps to say
how, at such altitudes,
the earth extends clear to the rim of its fish bowl,
where it greys and shifts absently,
as if it were ocean floor.

Seen in the plane's window,
things below take the size of the pores of my hand
writing, then resting on this paper, giantly.
Below, everything is familiar only by similitude.
Cars move like these
lines of type, backing up, turning
careful corners by signals I knew by heart
but could not see from where I sat.

Such distances are managed
only by acts of pure invention:
by turning parking lots
to postage stamps,
and swimming pools into cheap brooches,
green with inlaid glass.
The cloverleaves — beautiful, occasional —
are, each, a curl of hair
lying in the dust on the desk.

Some features are difficult to name.
I remember that I could not answer
why the cities would begin to gather themselves here
and then, there, let go,
draining off into a fur of trees.
And when suddenly
clouds blocked the view,
and voices called my attention to the fact of landing,
all likeness stopped.
Through dense white air,
I was taken down swallowing.
At what angle to descend was not in my control.
Yellow broad lines on the pavement
had told the pilot where to berth the plane, exactly.
I remember that everyone followed a slow rhythm
down the aisle finally stepping
out onto the windy ladder touching
ground under an evening sky.

In the glassed room beyond the gate,
amidst the moving strange close shapes,
I rushed to find your shape: the chest,
legs, arms, familiar hair, cheeks, eyes of it.
I remember how your hands opened out
and took the very size of mine.

Sitting here writing,
I follow signals that I know by heart,
devising lines of type,
backing up
in order to relate
my uncontrolled descent into that room.
I listen for you. I expect you home.

Northfield Night

Our eyes, like lions, like fire,
catch this sky.

A diamond black new sky
is on us, drowning

Zion's stars. Now it blows down
snow, crowning us

with a wild cloud, with a white flame.
This is the ground we share.

After the Hurricane

Fresh-sawed limbs,
leaves limp, branches
wait curbside for the refuse truck.
The mash of tree pulp
in the gutter, as I walk past,
smells like shreds of wound.
Last night they bled like cut flesh;
their blood sweetens the morning
faintly now.

At the trolley stop
I remember my dream:
attendants with a stretcher
came down our driveway
into the backyard.
A wraith under the sheet,
white limbs loose like sticks —
I recognize my neighbor,
the one who rails, who cuts
people with her words.
Her bleached body is limp,
as if drowned, or spent.
I gather her up, sheets,
skin, bones,
and cradle her.

Then I spread a cover out
over the whole yard,
like a robe of fur,
as if I were making a bed.

January Noon

From an old failure these phoenixes
fly out, from brown pools shining
where cloud white snatches move.
Noon cats sunsleep on January walls;
all along, in glassed sky patches of old road
winter birds dip and glance.

Wet in this hour, these glare spots
darken after, and close dry,
but will next day crack, and sun
with phoenixes again
from these depressions,
from the ground's brown eyes,
while cats, puffed fat in sleep,
noon on these silent walls.

Yet New to Grief

Black overhead,
the dream-cast sky
yet showers down
its birds, flowers, stars, brides, chalices.
Purple-robed young men,
wild beards heavenwards,
fly like meteors, freely,
among the timeless moons.

These emblems cry out.
They answer shrill,
lighting like hawks,
gold and silver glinting from their wings.
They peer through the blind windows of the room
where I lie rigorous as if in state.
Breaking and entering then
at my mere eyelid's beckoning
they scatter in search across my body;
their claws shine as they peck and pick.

They hover to untie a neckpiece,
to loosen, ceremoniously,
the linens from my unknowing face.
Then with blood-red stares
they peer down into the mirror of my open eye.
They shriek to see
the buried bits of my mind's bone,
its bright glass yet reflecting
those stars, brides, chalices.
These emblems are sent for my soul's recovery.

January: Crane's Beach

It is the new year in a new world
and today I am the only one along its shore.
I am walking a winter-clear beach westward to Ipswich
where I have never been.

Beside me the sea forces
its waves over on themselves,
their crumbling edges swollen
thick with ice like summer slush.
Out far the steel surface moves
shadowed lime inside.
Nothing is what it seems.
Only the rocks look familiar —
grey and warm like summer.
Grey ice, like broken pieces of sky
scatter the shore
as far as the eye can see.

I climb into the dunes
to lie down and look up at the sky.
On my back, as if underwater,
I remember the deep soundlessness
of children's swimming, their legs like snakes
wavering towards the lime-white roof,
then plunging down again towards me,
making it clear to the ocean floor and back,
thin legs and hair willowing
as they thrash down fountains of white air.
Following them I slip up,
pierce the watery shell, breaking out into sky,
where summer sailfish rock at their loose lines,

and swimmers color the float
like birds in a bright flock.
Or like a flock of flowers.
I remember the day the wind took
the children's beachball out
and I swam after it,
the wind pushing it seaward
just a little faster than I could swim.
I tired suddenly and looked back.
The lifeguard was standing on shore
beside my small daughter watching me;
the water pulled and I felt my roots
loosening from the air.
I swam in, slowly, full of fear.

The wind bites. It lifts the sand.
This winter ocean, here draining off into dunes,
bears the old rains of transatlantic summers.
Far mountains, cities, gardens of Europe fill this basin,
and this ice bears traces of those distances:
lemonade poured from a glass,
cold now and salt.

I get up and start out again.
Across the bay, dry wooden houses
climb the black bank in a vacant toy arrangement
that no one plays with.
Ahead, the low small sun drifts
as in an arctic photograph —
a dim, yellow light
gathered round with moisture.
The wind drives sand into the sun's face,
carrying darkness with it, westward,
towards Ipswich where I have never been.

POETRY FROM ALICE JAMES BOOKS